MY EARLY
MORNING CRY

MY EARLY MORNING CRY

Berta Kai

XULON PRESS

Xulon Press
2301 Lucien Way #415
Maitland, FL 32751
407.339.4217
www.xulonpress.com

Printed in the United States of America.

ISBN-13: 978-1-66280-645-2
Ebook ISBN-13: 978-1-6628-0646-9

TABLE OF CONTENTS

PREFACE

ON OCTOBER 13, 2007, A GROUP OF PEOPLE decided to start a prayer line. We had observed that many of our church members were praying on the telephone with friends from other churches. It was then, after thinking about it, that we talked to our pastor, who decided that we would start praying together as a church. We began praying every morning at 5 AM and every evening at 8:30 PM. We have done this for the last thirteen years, and it is still ongoing. Over the years we have consistently cried out to the Lord in prayer for:

a) the Word of God to reach the ends of the earth.
b) the end time harvest
c) the family—growth of children, marriages, godly parenting, salvation, wholeness, and sound-mindedness
d) church growth—both numerical and spiritual
e) evangelism
f) Nations of the world—leadership, stability, open doors for the gospel of the kingdom

g) the church of Jesus (the body of Christ)—persecution, the sick and shut in, widows, church projects, impact on the world

h) the leading of the Holy Spirit

Most importantly we do not relent in reminding ourselves that Jesus Christ has won the battle. He has led captivity captive and we are more than conquerors in whatever we do.

At the end of these sections, we end with an encouraging word from our dear Pastor Lawrence Kennedy, who always has a "NOW WORD" from the holy Scripture that is able to help you as you go through the many challenges of the day.

Our 5AM time with the Lord is very powerful. His agenda is unpredictable. Sometimes it is warfare; other times it may be praise and worship. Because His thoughts and His ways are not like ours, we are always open to the leading of His Spirit.

It is a beautiful thing to wake up early in the morning and come into the presence of your true love. You can tell him everything and anything. You can cry, sing, shout, and He never judges you. In the presence of the Almighty God, the King of kings, the creator of the universe, our 5AM cry ascends like a sweet-smelling fragrance into His ears and nostrils. He not only hears, He also answers. He meets us there.

We refer to our prayer telephone line as "OUR LIFE LINE." Truly our lives are revived.

This is a collection of Scriptures that we have used during prayer, and I just like to share and encourage others to use them, too. When you can, EARLY MORNING PRAYER TIME is one of the best times to meet and spend time with the Lord Jesus.

FOREWORD

I FEEL SO HONORED TO PEN DOWN THE FORE-
word for this book. I salute Pastor Bertha Kai for daring
to step in the waters when many people are procrasti-
nating on what to do to advance the Kingdom of God in
these end times. The Early Morning Cry is a compilation
of prayer points sent out as flames from the faithful intercessors of Bethel World Outreach Ministries—Atlanta to
the throne room of heaven. This is in line with the words
spoken by David in Psalm 63:1: "Oh Lord, you are my
God, early will I seek you. My soul thirsts for you, my
flesh longs for you..."

Early in the morning is the best time to activate your
organs of interaction with the realm of the Spirit; to
petition heaven and sense the impulses of the spirit, to
know both what God is speaking and how God is moving.
Together with the body of intercessors, we have seen man-
ifestations of answers to prayers. The Early Morning
Cry comes from sacrifice. The Lord Jesus has given us
enduring grace to come together on the prayer line seven
days a week as watchmen on the wall, to stand in the gap

on behalf of the Body of Christ. The love of God compels us to go an extra mile. We draw from the throne of grace divine energy that grants us longevity in seeking His face. We have come to the realization that God has created divine strategies that are resident within us, which enable us to tap into what He is doing because He does not want us to live in ignorance. He says, "If you seek me, you will find me." The prayer points in this book are a product of spiritual hunger, wanting more from the Lord, and desiring to be intimate with Him.

By spending time in the presence of the Lord in the early morning, the dew of heaven has settled on us and the Lord has empowered us to paralyze every architect of conflict, confusion, and hostility that may try to derail us from our mandate: to win the lost at all cost.

As you read this book, I ask you to pray the prayer points and watch and see what the Lord will do in your life. We are the generation that will birth the end time revival for a great harvest of souls before the Lord raptures the Church. We have refused to walk in fear—we walk by faith. Let the Lord arise and let the enemies of the cross be scattered, in Jesus's name.

Dr. Pastor Judith Imoite
Intercessory prayer coordinator
Bethel World Outreach Ministries Atlanta

Coming Into His Presence

Scripture

> But when Christ came as high priest of the good things that are now already here, he went through the greater and more perfect tabernacle that is not made with human hands, that is to say, is not a part of this creation. He did not enter by means of the blood of goats and calves; but he entered the Most Holy Place once for all by his own blood, thus obtaining eternal redemption. The blood of goats and bulls and the ashes of a heifer sprinkled on those who are ceremonially unclean sanctify them so that they are outwardly clean. How much more, then, will the blood of Christ, who through the eternal Spirit offered himself unblemished to God, cleanse our consciences from acts that lead to death, so that we may serve the living God!
> (Hebrews 9:11)

+ We should not fear eternity because Jesus has already made an atonement for us.
+ Jesus brought everything to completion through His sacrifice on the cross.
+ Jesus was offered once and for all, so let us enter with gratitude for the blood of Jesus that has enabled us to be called the sons of God.

Scripture:

Humble yourselves, therefore, under God's mighty hand, that he may lift you up in due time. Cast all your anxiety on him because he cares for you.
(1 Peter 5:6

+ We should humble ourselves before God even as we partake in His calling.
+ We should cast our burdens, fears, inadequacies, and worries to God; put pride aside.

Encouragements

Scripture:
> Be strong and of good courage, do not fear
> nor be afraid of them; for the Lord your
> God, He is the One who goes with you. He
> will not leave you nor forsake you.
> (Deuteronomy 31:6 NKJV)

+ Anytime, we rely on our efforts, we become weary.
  So let us boast in the Lord and not be panic stricken.

Scripture :
> As soon as Jesus heard the word that was
> spoken, He said to the ruler of the syna-
> gogue, "Do not be afraid; only believe."
> Mark 5:36 NKJV

+ Do not be afraid; we need to believe.

Scripture:

> In that day you shall not be shamed for any of your deeds In which you transgress against Me; For then I will take away from your midst Those who rejoice in your pride, And you shall no longer be haughty In My holy mountain.
> (Zephaniah 3:11 NKJV)

+ Let us use faith to declare what we need from God.

Scripture:

> **For indeed the gospel was preached to us as well as to them; but the word which they heard did not profit them, not being mixed with faith in those who heard it.**
> *(Hebrews 4:2 NKJV)*

+ We get the rest of God through our belief in God (faith).
+ Let us therefore believe in God. No need to worry, for He is a miracle worker. He knows all our needs.
+ Cast every care upon the Lord and walk humbly before Him.
+ Jesus is not insensitive by Himself; He is among us and is always working. He is not unjust to forget

your labor of love. Whatever your hands find, do it with all your heart.

+ Submit to God. Resist the devil and he will flee from you. The devil seeks those he can devour, so put on the whole armor of God (faith).

+ Trust in the Lord and lean not on your own understanding. Many things happen to us, but God tells us not to fret, for He is with us. When the Israelites were in the desert, God protected them by cloud during the day, and by fire during the night.

+ We will have fear about ourselves, or fear because of the circumstances.

+ There are people in the Bible who also faced fear in given situations. For instance, Moses was not ready to face Pharaoh because of fear. But God gave him a rod, and a staff, and Aaron as a spokesman; He therefore gave Moses all he needed.

+ When David was anointed as king, many times he was faced with fear and had to really fight for that position. When he was being sought by King Saul, he had moments of fear and had to depend on God.

Scripture:

The Lord is my shepherd; I shall not want.
He makes me lie down in green pastures;
He leads me beside the still waters. He restores my soul; He leads me in the paths

of righteousness For His name's sake. Yea, though I walk through the valley of the shadow of death, I will fear no evil; For You are with me; Your rod and Your staff, they comfort me. You prepare a table before me in the presence of my enemies; You anoint my head with oil; My cup runs over. Surely goodness and mercy shall follow me All the days of my life; And I will dwell in the house of the Lord Forever. (Psalms 23:1

Scripture:

The Lord is my light and my salvation; Whom shall I fear? The Lord is the strength of my life; Of whom shall I be afraid? When the wicked came against me To eat up my flesh, My enemies and foes, They stumbled and fell. Though an army may encamp against me, My heart shall not fear; Though war may rise against me, In this I will be confident. One thing I have desired of the Lord , That will I seek: That I may dwell in the house of the Lord All the days of my life, To behold the beauty of the Lord , And to inquire in His temple. For in the time of trouble He shall hide me in His pavilion; In the secret place of His tabernacle He shall

hide me; He shall set me high upon a rock. And now my head shall be lifted up above my enemies all around me; Therefore I will offer sacrifices of joy in His tabernacle; I will sing, yes, I will sing praises to the Lord. Hear, O Lord , when I cry with my voice! Have mercy also upon me, and answer me. When You said, "Seek My face," My heart said to You, "Your face, Lord , I will seek." Do not hide Your face from me; Do not turn Your servant away in anger; You have been my help; Do not leave me nor forsake me, O God of my salvation. When my father and my mother forsake me, Then the Lord will take care of me. Teach me Your way, O Lord, And lead me in a smooth path, because of my enemies. Do not deliver me to the will of my adversaries; For false witnesses have risen against me, And such as breathe out violence. I would have lost heart, unless I had believed That I would see the good- ness of the Lord In the land of the living. Wait on the Lord; Be of good courage, And He shall strengthen your heart; Wait, I say, on the Lord!
(Psalms 27:1

+ The lord is our light and salvation, so let us acknowledge this through prayer. We should not fear men or the situations we go through. David remembered that it was God who had helped him to kill the lions and the bears while taking care of the sheep. He therefore knew that through God's strength he would kill the giants with just a stone. God will do the same with us.
+ Wait upon the Lord and be of good courage, even as we wait on Him.
+ God wants us to use His Word for every situation in our lives. From Genesis to Revelation, all those who called upon the lord were guided and protected. God always revealed His revelation upon them for as long as they acknowledged His name.
+ When in a hard situation, do not be disturbed by it. Remember the Lord and call on Him, for He is great and fights our battles.

Scripture:

> But now, thus says the Lord , who created you, O Jacob, And He who formed you, O Israel: "Fear not, for I have redeemed you; I have called you by your name; You are Mine. (Isaiah 43:1 NKJV)

+ Lift up your head in the midst of the problems, and pray that everywhere we go we become givers, for God has already taken away our shame and pain.

+ In Deuteronomy 4:29, we are told to seek the Lord and we will find Him. Fear cannot abide if we seek the Lord with all our hearts, minds, and souls.

+ May you receive the grace to serve Him in truth and God will honor you. At times, the circumstances you are facing today are for the glory of God to be revealed.

Scripture:

Now after Jesus was born in Bethlehem of Judea in the days of Herod the king, behold, wise men from the East came to Jerusalem, saying, "Where is He who has been born King of the Jews? For we have seen His star in the East and have come to worship Him." When Herod the king heard this, he was troubled, and all Jerusalem with him. And when he had gathered all the chief priests and scribes of the people together, he inquired of them where Christ was to be born. So they said to him, "In Bethlehem of Judea, for thus it is written by the prophet: 'But you, Bethlehem, in the land of Judah, Are not the least among the rulers of Judah; For out of you shall come a Ruler Who will shepherd My people Israel.' " Then Herod, when he had secretly called the wise men, determined from them what time the star appeared. And he sent them to Bethlehem and said, "Go and search carefully for the young Child, and when you have found Him, bring back word to me, that I may come and worship Him also." When they heard the king, they departed; and behold, the star which they had seen in the East went before them, till it came and stood over where the young Child was. When they saw the star, they rejoiced with great joy. And when they had come into the house, they saw the young Child with Mary His mother, and fell down and worshiped Him. And when they had opened their treasures, they presented gifts to Him: gold, frankincense, and myrrh. Then, being divinely warned in a dream that they should not return to Herod, they departed for their own country another way. Now when they had departed, behold, an angel of the Lord appeared to Joseph in a dream, saying, "Arise, take the young Child and His mother, flee to Egypt, and stay there until I bring you word; for Herod will seek the young Child to destroy Him." When he arose, he took the young Child and His mother by night and departed for Egypt, and was there until the death of Herod, that it might be fulfilled which was spoken by the Lord through the prophet, saying, "Out of Egypt I called My Son." Then Herod, when he saw that he was deceived by the wise men, was exceedingly angry; and he sent forth and put to death all the male children who were in Bethlehem and in all its districts, from two years old and under, according to the time which he had determined from the wise men. Then was fulfilled what was spoken by Jeremiah the prophet, saying: "A voice was heard in Ramah, Lamentation, weeping, and great mourning, Rachel weeping for her children, Refusing to be comforted, Because they are no more." Now when Herod was dead, behold, an angel of the Lord appeared in a dream to Joseph in Egypt, saying, "Arise, take the young Child and His mother, and go to the land of Israel, for those who sought the young Child's life are dead." Then he arose, took the young Child and His mother, and came into the land of Israel. But when he heard that Archelaus was reigning over Judea instead of his father Herod, he was afraid to go there. And being warned by God in a dream, he turned aside into the region of Galilee. And he came and dwelt in a city called Nazareth, that it might be fulfilled which was spoken by the prophets, "He shall be called a Nazarene." (Matthew 2:1

- Nothing is impossible for God, just like the angel told Mary.
- Always sow your seed of faith, and do not despise any small beginning. Get up and plant.
- When you step up, God brings a breakthrough.

Scripture:

Peace I leave with you, My peace I give to you; not as the world gives do I give to you. Let not your heart be troubled, neither let it be afraid. (John 14:27 NKJV)

- God gives us the peace that is different from the peace that the world gives. Therefore let us be confident that He will never leave us nor forsake us.

+ We should not be paralyzed by fear, for Jesus is in control.

+ Build your house on the rock (Jesus Christ) for He never fails.

+ Allow Jesus to be your "Facebook." Keep Him in your mind all the time, for what you keep is what you reproduce.

+ What you set before you is what you reproduce. Look up to Jesus; you will not be put to shame. See Gen. 30:39.

+ Testimonies solidify our faith; do not allow the enemy to divide your faith.

Scripture:

But know this, that in the last days perilous times will come: For men will be lovers of themselves, lovers of money, boasters, proud, blasphemers, disobedient to parents, unthankful, unholy, unloving, unforgiving, slanderers, without self-control, brutal, despisers of good, traitors, headstrong, haughty, lovers of pleasure rather than lovers of God, having a form of godliness but denying its power. And from such people turn away!
(2 Timothy 3:1)

- Let us not be abusive or disobedient; let us not be liars, fornicators, gossipers, or lovers of money, but instead have a heart of gratitude and glorify God's name.
- In Philippians 2:3 we learn of humility. We shouldn't consider ourselves better than others. Let us not just look to our own interests—our attitude should be Christ-like, for He took the nature of a servant.
- Jesus was obedient even to the point of death, and God exalted Him and gave Him a name above every name. As He did the humbling, God did the exaltation. God resists the proud and gives grace to the humble. (James 4:6; 1 Pet. 5:5-6)
- Colossians 4 reminds us to work passionately at whatever our hands find. Work with all your heart and from it you will receive an inheritance.

Scripture:

> For the law was given through Moses, but grace and truth came through Jesus Christ. (John 1:17 NKJV)

- Whenever we are faced with a hard situation, we need to shout "Grace, grace!" Any hindrance, opposition, or obstacle before us is not impossible for

God. Let's just shout "Grace, grace!" for His grace is sufficient.

+ Grace is therefore complete rest and peace. It brings us joy.
+ Strive at all times to enter God's rest.

Scripture:
> But Joshua the son of Nun and Caleb the son of Jephunneh, who were among those who had spied out the land, tore their clothes; and they spoke to all the congregation of the children of Israel, saying: "The land we passed through to spy out is an exceedingly good land.
> (Numbers 14:6

+ Let us therefore stand against every giant that comes against us in the name of Jesus.

Scripture:
> The angel of the Lord encamps all around those who fear Him, And delivers them.
> (Psalms 34:7 NKJV)

+ We are protected by God at all times, even many times we rarely see. God has surrounded us with an angelic host of protection. We shouldn't, therefore, succumb to fear, for we are never alone.

Scripture

> Pride ends in humiliation, while humility brings honor. If you assist a thief, you only hurt yourself. You are sworn to tell the truth, but you dare not testify. Fearing people is a dangerous trap, but trusting the Lord means safety. Many seek the ruler's favor, but justice comes from the Lord . The righteous despise the unjust; the wicked despise the godly.
> (Proverbs 29:23)

✦ A humble spirit brings honor. In whatever we do, let us seek justice from the Lord and not from men. If you humble yourself, God will lift you up.

Scripture:

> The Lord is my light and my salvation— so why should I be afraid? The Lord is my fortress, protecting me from danger, so why should I tremble? When evil people come to devour me, when my enemies and foes attack me, they will stumble and fall.
> (Psalms 27:1)

+ We are the children of God. He is our light and our salvation, so let us trust in the Lord.

Scripture:

> For the sin of this one man, Adam, caused death to rule over many. But even greater is God's wonderful grace and his gift of righteousness, for all who receive it will live in triumph over sin and death through this one man, Jesus Christ.
> (Romans 5:17 NLT)

+ We have received salvation through the fullness of His grace, so let us clothe ourselves in the clothes of righteousness, reigning in this life through Jesus Christ.
+ God is for us. All things work together for the good of those who love Him. God is at work.
+ Potiphar's wife lied, and though everything seemed to work against Joseph, that was a good thing in the long run; God wanted to connect him to the throne of Pharaoh.
+ Always use your fruit of self-control and righteousness and see God, in His divine timing, fulfill His purpose.
+ God can elevate you; He will give you double because He predestined you, He called you, and

He chose you. Even if others disqualify you, those who trust in the Lord always get fulfilment. God justifies and glorifies them.

+ Do not be afraid—God is for and with you even in your struggles. No one can condemn us. Jesus is at the right-hand side of God interceding for us.

+ In our weaknesses, we might not know how to pray, but the Holy Spirit intercedes for us in accordance with God's will.

+ Your defender is strong. Depend on God; stand firm on His promises. Be like the Shunamite woman who trusted in the Lord—she did not fear, for she knew God was in control.

+ Trust in God and walk in His revelation. Whatever you want, start seeing it, imagining it, for you are an overcomer. If God took care of the Israelites at the Red Sea, and then the desert, then let Him defend you, for He has the best plan.

+ God reverses curses to blessings, so do not fight for yourself. Hold your peace and leave the battle for God. If you want to overcome, do not overcome evil for evil; overcome evil with good.

Scripture

He said, "Listen, all you people of Judah and Jerusalem! Listen, King Jehoshaphat! This is what the Lord says: Do not be afraid! Don't be discouraged by this mighty army, for the battle is not yours, but God's. Tomorrow, march out against them. You will find them coming up through the ascent of Ziz at the end of the valley that opens into the wilderness of Jeruel. But you will not even need to fight. Take your positions; then stand still and watch the Lord's victory. He is with you, O people of Judah and Jerusalem. Do not be afraid or discouraged. Go out against them tomorrow, for the Lord is with you!" (2 Chronicles 20:15)

+ We get tormented because of fear and disbelief. In Isaiah 46:3, God assures you that He will help you. He chose you; He will uphold us. He knows us well from the time of conception and still takes care of us even in old age.

+ God will always sustain us. He will carry you and rescue you. Nothing compares to the love of God, for He is awesome and more than sufficient.

+ In John 14:27 we are reminded to walk in the peace of God. He created you for a purpose and will keep and uphold you. He never slumbers, so speak of your blessings in faith. When you speak life, you will experience life.

+ God comforts and blesses us so that we can do the same to others.

Scripture

> But the angel said, "Don't be afraid, Zechariah! God has heard your prayer. Your wife, Elizabeth, will give you a son, and you are to name him John. You will have great joy and gladness, and many will rejoice at his birth, for he will be great in the eyes of the Lord. He must never touch wine or other alcoholic drinks. He will be filled with the Holy Spirit, even before his birth."
> (Luke 1:13)

Scripture

> As he considered this, an angel of the Lord appeared to him in a dream. "Joseph, son of David," the angel said, "do not be afraid to take Mary as your wife. For the child within her was conceived by the Holy Spirit.
> (Matthew 1:20 NLT)

+ In these two chapters there are three aspects depicted: assurance, identity, and purpose. In the first reading, when the angel appeared to Zechariah, the son was the assurance, John was the identity, and the purpose was preparing the way for salvation of the people.

+ When the angel Gabriel appeared to Mary, the Holy Spirit was the assurance, Jesus was the identity, and the purpose was to save the people from their sins.

+ These births are unusual, since the names of the children were pronounced before birth. These sons were also to be a fulfilment of God's plan. Both sons were filled with the Holy Spirit. They had disciples in their ministry, and their first names began with J. The two fulfilled God's purpose and were great in God's sight. They prepared people for God.

+ Zachariah and Mary believed and were not afraid. Let us therefore thank God for the savior that was sent to redeem us from sins in prayer.

Scripture

The soldiers took Jesus into the courtyard of the governor's headquarters (called the Praetorium) and called out the entire regiment.
(Mark 15:16 NLT)

+ We have been called to preach the gospel to all the creatures, to spread the good news.

+ Let us therefore thank God that we do not need to err because we know our assurance in identity and purpose, and that His grace should guide us not to be fearful.

Scripture

> So faith comes from hearing, that is, hearing the Good News about Christ.
> (Romans 10:17 NLT)

+ Faith comes through hearing. The Bible is full of promises, but we have to step out.
+ We have to put confidence in Him. God gave us promises to possess; so remove any destructive thought and look to Jesus.
+ Naaman's servant advised his master to obey. He responded with calmness and told him to do as instructed. We should also be calm and obedient. Everything we have was provided long before we were born. After the fall of man, Jesus came and died for us and brought restoration to the achievement.
+ Salvation is a gift that is already provided. No need to fear! Whatever you ask in faith, you already receive (it is being manifested in the spiritual realm). At its divine time, you will see it, for God has already provided it.

+ Therefore, as we wait for His manifestation, we should thank Him. Let us work hard to restructure our minds to work so that we enter the rest of God.

+ Always count on your blessings; always go back and see the hand of God's favor. God will get you out of bondage and depression and give you joy. Just believe and trust in His deliverance.

+ God is our portion. As we speak life, He sends His hands of favor and courage upon us. We shall not die, but live and confess the glory of God.

+ As a wise man's heart guides his mouth, so let your speech be guided by your heart.

Scripture
(Read Exodus 16)

+ The Israelites' freedom came from the Lord. God loves us deeply, mainly because of His character and not because of who we are.

+ In Deuteronomy 7:6, He refers to us as a holy people. God chose us out of the earth to be His treasured possession. Out of the least, He chose us, because of the love He had for us and the oath He had sworn with our forefathers, for He is a covenant-keeping God. Therefore, God has redeemed us from the bondage and wickedness of sin and will not change His mind.

- We are redeemed and blessed. Scatter seeds of kindness, joy, happiness, and peace wherever you go and be a blessing to others.
- When faced with fear, remember the Lord; that is where your victory lies. When you see the ugly, call on Him. Eventually you will see it and it shall be good in your eyes.
- God made us in His image and told us to go multiply and become a blessing, even in the midst of darkness. Learn to lift people up, and if you can't bless them, do not hurt them.

Scripture

The Lord is my light and my salvation— so why should I be afraid? The Lord is my fortress, protecting me from danger, so why should I tremble? When evil people come to devour me, when my enemies and foes attack me, they will stumble and fall. Though a mighty army surrounds me, my heart will not be afraid. Even if I am attacked, I will remain confident. The one thing I ask of the Lord — the thing I seek most— is to live in the house of the Lord all the days of my life, delighting in the Lord 's perfections and meditating in his Temple. For he will conceal me there when troubles

come; he will hide me in his sanctuary. He will place me out of reach on a high rock. Then I will hold my head high above my enemies who surround me. At his sanctuary I will offer sacrifices with shouts of joy, singing and praising the Lord with music. Hear me as I pray, O Lord . Be merciful and answer me! My heart has heard you say, "Come and talk with me." And my heart responds, " Lord , I am coming." Do not turn your back on me. Do not reject your servant in anger. You have always been my helper. Don't leave me now; don't abandon me, O God of my salvation! Even if my father and mother abandon me, the Lord will hold me close. Teach me how to live, O Lord . Lead me along the right path, for my enemies are waiting for me. Do not let me fall into their hands. For they accuse me of things I've never done; with every breath they threaten me with violence. Yet I am confident I will see the Lord's goodness while I am here in the land of the living.
(Psalms 27:1)

+ Be encouraged that the Lord is your strength and protection. He hides you high upon a rock.

✦ Encourage yourself to wait on the Lord and be of good courage.

Scripture

And I am convinced that nothing can ever separate us from God's love. Neither death nor life, neither angels nor demons, neither our fears for today nor our worries about tomorrow—not even the powers of hell can separate us from God's love. No power in the sky above or in the earth below—indeed, nothing in all creation will ever be able to separate us from the love of God that is revealed in Christ Jesus our Lord. (Romans 8:38)

✦ The Lord commanded Joshua to be strong and courageous. He also assured him that no one would be able to stand against him for as long as he lived.

✦ Jesus said that His sheep listen to His voice. Therefore, let us listen to the voice of God. We are in the hands of God, and no one can snatch us away from Him. We are kept by the power of God.

✦ God is love. Whoever lives in love lives in God. There is no fear in love; therefore let us walk in love even towards others. Walk in the joy of the Lord, for His mercies and goodness will follow you.

+ Speak and experience life today, declare even the unseen things you want to see. Go after them and just appear. Over and beyond, may God supply all your needs.

Scripture

But when I am afraid, I will put my trust in you. I praise God for what he has promised. I trust in God, so why should I be afraid? What can mere mortals do to me? (Psalms 56:3)

+ The enemy uses worry, anxiety, fear, and doubt to fight us. The reality is what we spend time worrying about never happens. "What if" are words of defeat and doubts—let us be immersed in the Word of God and speak to ourselves, for God is the master of the skies, the ocean, and the sea.
+ When fear creeps in, put your trust in God.

Scripture

Don't worry about anything; instead, pray about everything. Tell God what you need, and thank him for all he has done. Then you will experience God's peace, which exceeds anything we can understand. His peace will

guard your hearts and minds as you live in
Christ Jesus.
(Philippians 4:6)

+ Be thankful for God's manifestation and calmness
in every area of storms we face in life.
+ Whichever the situation, speak to it. Our tongues
have power; what we profess comes into being.
Let us be careful with what we confess with our
tongues. As parents, let us be careful that what
comes out of our mouths aligns with the Word of
God. When your thoughts are negative, shut them
up. When you speak good words, the angels pick
them up to ensure they are manifested. Likewise,
when you speak negative, the devil picks up the
words to ensure they are effective.

Scripture

This is my command—be strong and courageous! Do not be afraid or discouraged.
For the Lord your God is with you wherever you go."
(Joshua 1:9 NLT)

+ We should walk by faith and not by sight. God
brings everything to completion, not merely halfway.

+ Everything has already been given; you only need to command it and see it being manifested.
+ Before he defeated Goliath, David referred to the God that had rescued him from the mouths of the bears and lions.
+ Elisha told his servants that they were surrounded with a larger army than that of their opponents.
+ God will always make a way; stop walking by sight and feelings. Walk on the promises of God, for they cannot be broken.
+ The blessings of God are rich. You are a speaking spirit, so scatter life in the midst of chaos. In so doing, fear has no place in your life.

Scripture

When you go through deep waters, I will be with you. When you go through rivers of difficulty, you will not drown. When you walk through the fire of oppression, you will not be burned up; the flames will not consume you.
(Isaiah 43:2 NLT)

+ The Israelites passed through the Red Sea and were not drowned by the waters. The Hebrew boys went through the fire but it did not burn them. Instead, those who threw them in the fire were burnt.

+ Jesus said to Lazarus's sisters that if they believed, they would see the glory of God.

+ Remember Philipians 4:13: **"I can do all things through Christ who strengthens me."**

+ God fights our battles whether they are physical, emotional, or spiritual, so let us ask God to fight all our battles as we cast all our cares to Jesus and also ask God to supply all our needs to us.

Scripture

And they were singing the song of Moses, the servant of God, and the song of the Lamb: "Great and marvelous are your works, O Lord God, the Almighty. Just and true are your ways, O King of the nations. Who will not fear you, Lord, and glorify your name? For you alone are holy. All nations will come and worship before you, for your righteous deeds have been revealed." (Revelation 15:3)

+ Fear is dangerous, but Jesus is always ready to fight for us. Let our songs resemble what is written in Revelation chapter 15—that we shall rejoice, for Jesus finally thrown into the bottomless pit.

+ Let us thank and praise God for the victory He has already promised to us.

Notes

Scripture:

> Therefore humble yourselves under the mighty hand of God, that He may exalt you in due time, casting all your care upon Him, for He cares for you.
> (1 Peter 5:6)

+ As we cast all the fears and worries at Jesus's feet, let us go with thanksgiving to God and also pray, for everyone else who has worries, fears, and anxieties, that God will deliver them.

Scripture:

> For indeed the gospel was preached to us as well as to them; but the word which they heard did not profit them, not being mixed with faith in those who heard it.
> (Hebrews 4:2 NKJV)

+ We have heard the gospel just like them; however, those who heard did not find the word relevant because they lacked faith.
+ We believe through faith. The rest of God comes upon us when we stand on His promises.

Scripture

> The Lord is my shepherd; I shall not want. He makes me lie down in green pastures; He leads me beside the still waters. He restores my soul; He leads me in the paths of righteousness For His name's sake. Yea, though I walk through the valley of the shadow of death, I will fear no evil; For You are with me; Your rod and Your staff, they comfort me. You prepare a table before me in the presence of my enemies; You anoint my head with oil; My cup runs over. Surely goodness and mercy shall follow me All the days of my life; And I will dwell in the house of the Lord Forever.
> (Psalms 23:1)

+ We see here that David fears no evil, for he knows that God is with him.
+ Jehoshaphat was a king who was faithful to God. It reached a point that when he was confronted

with fear, he turned his face to God. He had leaned that victory comes from the Lord, for He remains faithful to His word.

Scripture:

Now after Jesus was born in Bethlehem of Judea in the days of Herod the king, behold, wise men from the East came to Jerusalem, saying, "Where is He who has been born King of the Jews? For we have seen His star in the East and have come to worship Him." When Herod the king heard this, he was troubled, and all Jerusalem with him. And when he had gathered all the chief priests and scribes of the people together, he inquired of them where Christ was to be born. So they said to him, "In Bethlehem of Judea, for thus it is written by the prophet: 'But you, Bethlehem, in the land of Judah, Are not the least among the rulers of Judah; For out of you shall come a Ruler Who will shepherd My people Israel.'" Then Herod, when he had secretly called the wise men, determined from them what time the star appeared. And he sent them to Bethlehem and said, "Go and search carefully for the young Child, and when you have found Him, bring back word to me, that I may come and worship Him also." When they heard the king, they departed; and behold, the star which they had seen in the East went before them, till it came and stood over where the young Child was. When they saw the star, they rejoiced with great joy. And when they had come into the house, they saw the young Child with Mary His mother, and fell down and worshiped Him. And when they had opened their treasures, they presented gifts to Him: gold, frankincense, and myrrh. Then, being divinely warned in a dream that they should not return to Herod, they departed for their own country another way. Now when they had departed, behold, an angel of the Lord appeared to Joseph in a dream, saying, "Arise, take the young Child and His mother, flee to Egypt, and stay there until I bring you word; for Herod will seek the young Child to destroy Him." When he arose, he took the young Child and His mother by night and departed for Egypt, and was there until the death of Herod, that it might be fulfilled which was spoken by the Lord through the prophet, saying, "Out of Egypt I called My Son." Then Herod, when he saw that he was deceived by the wise men, was exceedingly angry; and he sent forth and put to death all the male children who were in Bethlehem and in all its districts, from two years old and under, according to the time which he had determined from the wise men. Then was fulfilled what was spoken by Jeremiah the prophet, saying: "A voice was heard in Ramah, Lamentation, weeping, and great mourning, Rachel weeping for her children, Refusing to be comforted, Because they are no more." Now when Herod was dead, behold, an angel of the Lord appeared in a dream to Joseph in Egypt, saying, "Arise, take the young Child and His mother, and go to the land of Israel, for those who sought the young Child's life are dead." Then he arose, took the young Child and His mother, and came into the land of Israel. But when he heard that Archelaus was reigning over Judea instead of his father Herod, he was afraid to go there. And being warned by God in a dream, he turned aside into the region of Galilee. And he came and dwelt in a city called Nazareth, that it might be fulfilled which was spoken by the prophets, "He shall be called a Nazarene."

(Matthew 2:1)

+ When Jesus was born in Bethlehem, Herod was tormented; he was troubled and argued that a great king could not come from the least tribe of Judah.

+ Herod hated the name of Jesus; he did not want to hear about it when the Maggi informed him about His birth. On the contrary, apostle Paul says he is not ashamed of the gospel, for in the gospel, the righteousness of God is revealed.

+ Herod tried to silence the will of God, but he did not manage. So let us pray for God to give us boldness like that of Paul, so that in our service to Him, we shall confidently profess the name of Jesus wherever we are without the spirit of fear in us.

+ Herod wanted to frustrate God's will and purpose by eliminating Jesus as a baby, so he decreed that all boys under age two be killed (See Job 42:2, Psalms 118:6).

+ Our unbelief hinders us from receiving God's blessings.

+ Without faith in God, it is impossible to please Him. The lepers' faith made them go into the city (see 2 Kings 7:1-12).

+ Where there is great faith, there is also a great reward. It is what prompted them to go to the Aramaean camp (an enemy camp). They dared, and through their faith, God revealed His power. The Aramaeans fled, for God had magnified their approaching steps to sound like chariots. They were scared and they left the camp, with all the supplies. God therefore worked in the favor of the lepers. The best way to experience God's blessings is to move in faith.

Scripture

For the law was given through Moses, but grace and truth came through Jesus Christ. (John 1:17 NKJV)

- To know God is to emulate Jesus. God sent Jesus to come and guide us to His righteousness.
- Paul prayed fervently when he was facing trials. He says that God's grace is made perfect in his weaknesses.

Scripture

Then He arose and rebuked the wind, and said to the sea, "Peace, be still!" And the wind ceased and there was a great calm. But He said to them, "Why are you so fearful? How is it that you have no faith?" (Mark 4:39)

+ The wind died down at His command. As Jesus spoke to the wind, the wave, and the storm, they calmed down.

Scripture:

> But Joshua the son of Nun and Caleb the son of Jephunneh, who were among those who had spied out the land, tore their clothes; and they spoke to all the congregation of the children of Israel, saying: "The land we passed through to spy out is an exceedingly good land.
> (Numbers 14:6)

+ Whatever you plant in your imagination matters. The power of life and death is in your tongue. When the spies were sent to Jericho, they came back complaining and grumbling; they were confessing death.
+ However, Joshua and Caleb were different, as they confessed hope, success, victory, life, and courage in the name of the Lord.

Prayer Points

Scripture
> Therefore humble yourselves under the
> mighty hand of God, that He may exalt you
> in due time, casting all your care upon Him,
> for He cares for you.
> (1 Peter 5:6)

+ Let us pray for all the individuals that make
  great decisions in every unit of authority, starting
  from the family bread-winners, for them not to
  worry or fear.

+ As we cast all the fears and worries at Jesus's feet,
  let us go with thanksgiving to God and pray that
  He delivers everyone else who has worries, fears,
  and anxieties.

Scripture:
> In that day you shall not be shamed for
> any of your deeds In which you transgress
> against Me; For then I will take away from

your midst Those who rejoice in your pride,
And you shall no longer be haughty In My
holy mountain.
(Zephaniah 3:11 NKJV)

- Let us proclaim blessings upon our children, let us put our fears aside and pray with faith as we speak the desires of our hearts upon our children to displace every weapon of darkness against them.
- Let us pray for God to take over the ailing kids, and restore their health

Scripture:

The Lord is my light and my salvation; Whom shall I fear? The Lord is the strength of my life; Of whom shall I be afraid? When the wicked came against me To eat up my flesh, My enemies and foes, They stumbled and fell. Though an army may encamp against me, My heart shall not fear; Though war may rise against me, In this I will be confident. One thing I have desired of the Lord, That will I seek: That I may dwell in the house of the Lord All the days of my life, To behold the beauty of the Lord, And to inquire in His temple. For in the time of trouble He shall hide me in His pavilion; In

the secret place of His tabernacle He shall hide me; He shall set me high upon a rock. And now my head shall be lifted up above my enemies all around me; Therefore I will offer sacrifices of joy in His tabernacle; I will sing, yes, I will sing praises to the Lord. Hear, O Lord, when I cry with my voice! Have mercy also upon me, and answer me. When You said, "Seek My face," My heart said to You, "Your face, Lord, I will seek." Do not hide Your face from me; Do not turn Your servant away in anger; You have been my help; Do not leave me nor forsake me, O God of my salvation. When my father and my mother forsake me, Then the Lord will take care of me. Teach me Your way, O Lord, And lead me in a smooth path, because of my enemies. Do not deliver me to the will of my adversaries; For false witnesses have risen against me, And such as breathe out violence. I would have lost heart, unless I had believed That I would see the goodness of the Lord In the land of the living. Wait on the Lord; Be of good courage, And He shall strengthen your heart; Wait, I say, on the Lord!
(Psalms 27:1)

+ Let us offer a prayer for all those who are going through fire—for God's grace and strength to see them through, and for them to receive the grace and comfort to trust in God for a turn around.
+ Let's speak the words of God's promises found in Psalm 27 over those going through fire.

Scripture:

2 Now after Jesus was born in Bethlehem of Judea in the days of Herod the king, behold, wise men from the East came to Jerusalem, saying, "Where is He who has been born King of the Jews? For we have seen His star in the East and have come to worship Him." When Herod the king heard this, he was troubled, and all Jerusalem with him. And when he had gathered all the chief priests and scribes of the people together, he inquired of them where the Christ was to be born. So they said to him, "In Bethlehem of Judea, for thus it is written by the prophet: 'But you, Bethlehem, in the land of Judah, Are not the least among the rulers of Judah; For out of you shall come a Ruler Who will shepherd My people Israel.'" Then Herod, when he had secretly called the wise men, determined from them what time the star

appeared. And he sent them to Bethlehem and said, "Go and search carefully for the young Child, and when you have found Him, bring back word to me, that I may come and worship Him also." When they heard the king, they departed; and behold, the star which they had seen in the East went before them, till it came and stood over where the young Child was. When they saw the star, they rejoiced with exceeding great joy. And when they had come into the house, they saw the young Child with Mary His mother, and fell down and worshiped Him. And when they had opened their treasures, they presented gifts to Him: gold, frankincense, and myrrh. Then, being divinely warned in a dream that they should not return to Herod, they departed for their own country another way. Now when they had departed, behold, an angel of the Lord appeared to Joseph in a dream, saying, "Arise, take the young Child and His mother, flee to Egypt, and stay there until I bring you word; for Herod will seek the young Child to destroy Him." When he arose, he took the young Child and His mother by night and departed for Egypt, and was there until the death of Herod, that it might be fulfilled which was spoken by the Lord through the prophet, saying, "Out of Egypt I called My Son." Then Herod, when he saw that he was deceived by the wise men, was exceedingly angry; and he sent forth and put to death all the male children who were in Bethlehem and in all its districts, from two years old and under, according to the time which he had determined from the wise men. Then was fulfilled what was spoken by Jeremiah the prophet, saying: "A voice was heard in Ramah, Lamentation, weeping, and great mourning, Rachel weeping for her children, Refusing to be comforted, Because they are no more." Now when Herod was dead, behold, an angel of the Lord appeared in a dream to Joseph in Egypt, saying, "Arise, take the young Child and His mother, and go to the land of Israel, for those who sought the young Child's life are dead." Then he arose, took the young Child and His mother, and came into the land of Israel. But when he heard that Archelaus was reigning over Judea instead of his father Herod, he was afraid to go there. And being warned by God in a dream, he turned aside into the

region of Galilee. And he came and dwelt
in a city called Nazareth, that it might be
fulfilled which was spoken by the prophets,
"He shall be called a Nazarene."
(Matthew 2:1)

+ Let us pray that the Holy Spirit helps us not to
  despise our humble beginnings.
+ Pray that the Holy Spirit will guide us to Jesus, and
  that we too can guide others to Him through the
  spirit inside of us.
+ Let us pray for the ministry of the Holy Spirit to
  be active in our lives.

Scripture:
Peace I leave with you, My peace I give to
you; not as the world gives do I give to you.
Let not your heart be troubled, neither let
it be afraid.
(John 14:27 NKJV)

+ Pray for the peace of God to be revealed to those
  who are called by God's name.
+ Pray that believers will have confidence in the
  peace of God and be willing to rest in that peace.

- Pray for believers who are being persecuted because of their faith, that they will find peace in God through their times of trial.

Scripture:
> Stand fast therefore in the liberty by which Christ has made us free, and do not be entangled again with a yoke of bondage. (Galatians 5:1 NKJV)

- Thank Jesus for giving us the freedom to reconnect with God and serve Him.

Scripture:
> For the law was given through Moses, but grace and truth came through Jesus Christ. (John 1:17 NKJV)

- Thank Jesus for showing us the way to the Father.
- Let us pray for all the saints and governments of the world, that mountains and obstacles will come down in the name of Jesus.

Scripture:
> Then He arose and rebuked the wind, and said to the sea, "Peace, be still!" And the wind ceased and there was a great calm. But

He said to them, "Why are you so fearful?
How is it that you have no faith?"
(Mark 4:39)

* Let's pray, believing this day that we are not walking
  in fear. Pray for calmness and peace of mind.

Scriptures:

So he answered, "Do not fear, for those who
are with us are more than those who are
with them." And Elisha prayed, and said,
"Lord , I pray, open his eyes that he may see."
Then the Lord opened the eyes of the young
man, and he saw. And behold, the mountain was full of horses and chariots of fire
all around Elisha.
(2 Kings 6:16)

I sought the Lord, and He heard me, And
delivered me from all my fears.
(Psalms 34:4 NKJV)

The angel of the Lord encamps all around
those who fear Him, And delivers them.
(Psalms 34:7 NKJV)

You must not fear them, for the Lord your
God Himself fights for you.'
(Deuteronomy 3:22 NKJV)

- Let us Pray for God to open our eyes to perceive
  angelic protection and maintain our confidence.
- The Holy Spirit is here to help; let us present our
  early morning cry to God.

Scripture

And when I saw Him, I fell at His feet as
dead. But He laid His right hand on me,
saying to me, "Do not be afraid; I am the
First and the Last.
(Revelation 1:17 NKJV)

- Let us pray boldly asking for our needs and
  wants from the Lord, because nothing is impossible with Him.
- Let us commit all of our inadequacies, weaknesses,
  businesses, and relationships to the Lord. Pray to
  hear the voice of God, for He is the first and last.
  He is the Lord; He can do all things.

Scripture:

So Moses and Aaron went to Pharaoh and
did what the Lord had commanded them.

Aaron threw down his staff before Pharaoh
and his officials, and it became a serpent!
(Exodus 7:10 NLT)

+ Let us pray that the fear of God will lead us to obey
  Him and do the right thing.
+ Pray that the love and respect of God will lead us
  to obey rather than submitting to man.

Scripture

Pride ends in humiliation, while humility
brings honor. If you assist a thief, you only
hurt yourself. You are sworn to tell the truth,
but you dare not testify. Fearing people is a
dangerous trap, but trusting the Lord means
safety. Many seek the ruler's favor, but justice
comes from the Lord. The righteous despise
the unjust; the wicked despise the godly.
(Proverbs 29:23)

+ Pray that we continually trust in the Lord. Let us
  not fear men, for our strength is in the Lord Jesus.

Scripture

So faith comes from hearing, that is, hearing
the Good News about Christ.
(Romans 10:17 NLT)

+ Let us pray for God's grace to be loyal, faithful, and good, and to extend the same to our neighbors as well.

Scripture:
Read for yourself Exodus chapter 16

+ Let us Pray that God will give us strength and grace to remain on His way, and help us to come out of any fear which is still embedded in us.
+ Our children are our fears. We worry much about their health, education, peer influence, their future behavior, etc. Let us therefore stand in the gap, praying for them that God will deliver them from all the traps of the evil one and they will follow the way of the Lord. Pray that God will guide and protect them.
+ Pray for the nations of the world. As we enjoy the privileges, prosperity, and peace that prevails upon the land, pray to God to dismiss all the fears and intimidation in others.
+ Pray for the poor, the homeless, the addicts, and those who until today have not received salvation. God has given us the grace and we should not take it for granted. Let us put pride aside, for He is our shield and has carried us. We should remain grateful for every blessing He has bestowed upon us.

Scripture

> When doubts filled my mind, your comfort
> gave me renewed hope and cheer.
> (Psalms 94:19 NLT)

+ Let us thank God for His manifestation and ask Him to bring calmness into every area of storm that we face.
+ Speak the Word of God to every storm in your life.

ASSURANCE

Scripture:
> Be strong and of good courage, do not fear
> nor be afraid of them; for the Lord your
> God, He is the One who goes with you. He
> will not leave you nor forsake you."
> (Deuteronomy 31:6 NKJV)

+ God delivered the Israelites through the power of
His words. Moses also relied on the Word of God
to encourage the Israelites while in the desert.
+ God is working to bring out the best in every one
of us. His Word has not changed. He is above
everything.

Scripture:
> For I, the Lord your God, will hold your
> right hand, Saying to you, 'Fear not, I will
> help you.' "Fear not, you worm Jacob, You
> men of Israel! I will help you," says the

Lord and your Redeemer, the Holy One
of Israel.
(Isaiah 41:13)

+ God is with you. In Psalm 46:1 we are assured of
God's refuge.
+ God does not want us to fear but trust in Him, our
refuge, our stronghold.

Scripture

For indeed the gospel was preached to us
as well as to them; but the word which they
heard did not profit them, not being mixed
with faith in those who heard it.
(Hebrews 4:2 NKJV)

+ God is our portion. When we enter His rest, we
find peace in carrying out His work.
+ God says in His Word that He is always where His
servants are; so when we follow the Word of God,
we find Him.
+ We do His will when we feed the poor, attend to
and heal the sick, comfort the brokenhearted, visit
the orphanages.
+ When you serve the Lord, He will honor you. He
is the same God that honored Mordecai in the eyes
of his enemy.

+ You are God's responsibility. There is a portion for you; all the doors will open for you as we learn to serve Him in humility.
+ Nothing is in vain. God takes note of everything we do and takes us on to a bigger stage as we walk in boldness, faith, and victory.

Scripture:

The Lord is my shepherd; I shall not want. He makes me lie down in green pastures; He leads me beside the still waters. He restores my soul; He leads me in the paths of righteousness For His name's sake. Yea, though I walk through the valley of the shadow of death, I will fear no evil; For You are with me; Your rod and Your staff, they comfort me. You prepare a table before me in the presence of my enemies; You anoint my head with oil; My cup runs over. Surely goodness and mercy shall follow me All the days of my life; And I will dwell in the house of the Lord Forever.
(Psalms 23:1)

+ The Lord is our deliverer and strength; call on Him in every situation.

Read Psalm 27.

✦ Our God is KING of kings, so wait on the Lord, for He will strengthen us and take us from one level to another.

Scripture:

> But you are a chosen generation, a royal priesthood, a holy nation, His own special people, that you may proclaim the praises of Him who called you out of darkness into His marvelous light.
> (1 Peter 2:9)

✦ We are a chosen generation: Christians, children of God, a holy nation.
✦ Remain assured that what God's Word says about you is true and must all come to pass. We have been called out of darkness into His marvelous light. Therefore, let's remain in the light.

Acknowledgments

This book is dedicated to my Holy Father who has always been, and will ever be, my Heavenly Father.

It is dedicated also to the Bethel Atlanta (now Harvesters Intercontinental Ministries International) Prayer Line Family.

I also acknowledge Pastor Lawrence E. Kennedy, Sr., head pastor, and Pastor Judith Imoite, head of prayer ministry at Bethel, as well as all the men and women for their steadfastness and dedication to prayer.

Special thanks to all who assisted in every way with the completion of this book.

Finally I dedicate this to Zuri, the joy of my heart; Caleb-Joel, who gave grandma his first $20.00 from his piggy bank to start the process; to Siata, my prescript editor—all my grandchildren. Special thanks to Samuel Hooke, Weata K., and my family and friends. So glad I've been blessed with you all in this project.

CPSIA information can be obtained
at www.ICGtesting.com
Printed in the USA
LVHW090430020221
678100LV00008B/105